Ketogenic Recipes

Very simple keto meals for everyone with illustration images

Celine King

TABLE OF CONTENT

Introduction

The ketogenic diet is a very low carb, high-fat, and moderate protein diet. The idea behind the ketogenic diet is that the liver will break down fatty acids into ketones, which can fuel the brain. Ketogenic diets are often prescribed for children with intractable epilepsy because they may experience seizure control while on this type of eating plan. There are many reasons to try a ketogenic diet, but the biggest reason is weight loss. This diet allows you to lose weight without training a lot, as your body burns fat for energy instead of carbohydrates. As a result, you can have more energy, feel better, and have fewer cravings.

An essential step in any diet is considering and establishing goals—thinking hard about being able to precisely articulate what you wish to achieve by getting started on a diet. Because of the temptations of food and treats that can cause us to watch out for health-wise, a keto diet is a fantastic option due to all of the ailments it can help prevent or supplement.

Most people can safely seek out the keto diet. Nonetheless, it is best to talk to a dietitian or doctor about any significant diet changes. It is the case for those with disabilities underlying it.

A successful treatment for people with drug-resistant epilepsy could be the keto diet.

While the diet can be ideal for people of any age, children, and people over the age of 50, infants may enjoy the most significant benefits as they can easily adhere to the diet.

Adolescents and adults, such as the modified Atkins diet or the low-glycemic index diet, can do better on a modified keto diet.

A health care provider should track closely; whoever is using a keto diet as a medication. A doctor and dietitian can monitor a person's progress, prescribe medications, and test for adverse effects.

The body processes fat differently from that it processes protein differently from that of carbohydrates. The Carbohydrate response to insulin is extreme. The protein response to insulin is moderate, and the fast response to the insulin is minimal. Insulin is the hormone that produces fat / conserves fat.

After you've planned out your protein and carbohydrates, eat fat. You can eat all the fat you want as long as you're not doing it to excess. But unlike Weight Watchers or other diet plans, you don't need to measure fat or count calories. Simply let your body tell you when you've had enough. If you eat fat until you're satiated, you won't have problems consuming too many calories. If you eat and still feel like you need to eat more – do it. Many beginners on keto get into trouble when they don't eat enough fat. Fasting can be incorporated into the keto diet if it's done correctly. Try out one of the intermittent fasting techniques to help accelerate and maintain weight loss after you're adapted to keto.

Electronic monitors can be beneficial to keep track of your progress at home. If you can afford it, you should get a blood sugar monitor and a ketone monitor. Track your fasting blood sugars and keep track of your ketones, ensuring they fall within the 1.5-3.0 mmol/dL range. Also, you may want to track your HDL and triglycerides. Home monitors can be used to do this and allow you to monitor progress more frequently and keep away from unnecessary trips to the doctor's office.

Lastly, remember to keep a journal. It's essential to keep track of your progress and helps you note not only how your triglycerides may be improving, but if you write down what you eat and find out you're not losing weight, it will make it easier to pinpoint problem areas where you can improve.

DINNER RECIPES

Beef and Eggplant Kebab

Preparation Time: 20 minutes

Cooking Time: 15 minutes

Serving: 4

Ingredients:

- 3 tbsp. oil
- 1/2 tsp. dried thyme
- 1/2 tsp. oregano
- 2 eggs (beaten)
- 1/2 eggplant
- 1/2 tsp. chili pepper (ground)

- 1/4 cup olive oil
- 4 garlic cloves (crushed)
- 1 cup parsley leaves (chopped)
- 1 lb. beef (minced)
- 1 tsp. salt
- 1/2 tsp. black pepper

Directions:

1. Cut the eggplant into thin slices of about half inch. Season with salt and set aside. Put minced meat in a large bowl, add thyme, eggs, chili pepper, onions, parsley, olive oil, garlic, salt, oregano, and black pepper.

2. Combine the mixture. Shape equal-sized patties with wet hands. Preheat a skillet over medium-high heat and grease with oil. Rinse the eggplant slices sprinkled with salt and pat dry with hand or paper towel. Thread eggplant slices and patties alternately onto skewers and place on the preheated skillet.

3. Flip the sides occasionally and cook for 15 minutes. Remove from the heat and garnish with parsley. Serve warm with low-carb pita bread.

Nutrition:

39g Fat 23g Protein 4g Net Carbs 465 Calories

Skin Salmon with Pesto Cauliflower Rice

Preparation Time: 20 minutes

Cooking Time: 20 minutes

Serving: 3

Ingredients:

- 3 cups frozen riced cauliflower
- 1/cup olive oil
- 1 lemon
- 1 scoop keto MCT powder
- 1/4 cup hemp hearts
- 3 garlic cloves
- 3 salmon fillets

- 1 tbsp. butter
- 1 tbsp. olive oil
- 1 tbsp. coconut amino
- 1 tsp. red boat fish sauce
- 1 cup basil leaves (chopped)
- 1/2 tsp. pink salt
- Pinch of salt

Directions:

1. Grease a dish with olive oil, add coconut amino and fish sauce. Pat dry the salmon fillets and place them on marinade with meat side down. Season the top with salt and set aside for about 20 minutes. Add the minced garlic, hemp hearts, lemon juice, basil, olive oil, MCT powder, and salt in a food processor.

2. Blend until it reaches a sauce-like consistency. Add olive oil to a large skillet and put it on the stove-top. Add the cauliflower rice and cook until crisp-tender. Scoop out a few spoons of pesto you prepared and add into the skillet. Season with pink salt and stir until fully incorporated.

3. Place a skillet on medium heat and line with butter. Add the salmon with skin side down and cook for 5 minutes or until the crust browns. Flip the side and coat it with the remaining marinade. Sauté for about 2 minutes and remove from heat. Dish out the salmon and cauliflower rice. Top with pesto and serve warm.

Nutrition:

51 g Fat 33.8g Protein 10g Net Carbs 647 Calories

Chicken Enchilada Casserole

Preparation Time: 5 minutes

Cooking Time: 40 minutes

Serving: 6

Ingredients:

- 1/4 tsp. xanthan gum
- 1/2 tsp. onion powder
- 1 tsp. chili powder
- 1 tsp. cumin
- 1 tsp. garlic powder
- 1 tsp. oregano
- 6 lbs. chicken breast (boneless)
- 2 oz. black olives (slivered)
- 2 cups chicken broth
- 4 oz. green chilies
- 3/4 cup sour cream
- 1 cup cheddar cheese
- 3 tbsp. butter
- 1/2 tsp. pink Himalayan salt

Directions:

1. Place a large skillet over medium-high heat and add butter. Add the xanthan gum and allow thickening. Pour the chicken broth and stir through the xanthan gum. Allow cooking for two minutes. Sprinkle with salt, onion powder, olive, cumin, and oregano, and chilies. Stir thoroughly to combine.

2. Add the chicken and bring to boil. Low the flame and allow cooking for 20 minutes with the lid on. Stir occasionally to avoid sticking. Remove from heat once the chicken is fully cooked. Shred the cooked chicken into small chunks. Place a skillet over medium heat and add in the sour cream. Stir in the spices to taste and add the shredded chicken. Preheat the oven to 350°F. Season with cheddar cheese and transfer the skillet to the oven. Bake for 10 minutes or until the cheese melts. Serve warm with cauliflower rice or tortillas.

3. Keep in an airtight container to refrigerate for up to two weeks.

Nutrition:

20.7g Fat 27.8g Protein 4.5g Net Carbs 309 Calories

Preparation Time: 15 minutes

Cooking Time: 45 minutes

Serving: 10

Ingredients:

Base

- 2 pounds beef (minced)
- 3 celery sticks (chopped)
- 1 onion (chopped)
- 1 tbsp. dried oregano
- 2 garlic cloves (ground)
- 3 tbsp. olive oil

- 3 tbsp. tomato paste
- 1 cup beef stock
- 1/4 cup red wine vinegar
- 2 tbsp. dried thyme leaves
- 10 ounces green beans
- 1 tsp. salt

Topping

- 3 ounces butter
- 1 pinch of dried oregano
- 3 eggs (only yolk)
- 1/4 tsp. pepper (ground)

- 6 pounds florets of cauliflower
- 1 pinch of paprika
- 1/2 tsp. salt

Directions:

1. Put a large skillet over medium-high flame. Add olive oil, oregano, onion, celery, and garlic. Grill for 5 minutes or until the onion becomes translucent.
2. Add the minced beef and sprinkle salt. Stir occasionally till the meat begins to brown. Add tomato paste to the cooked meat and mix well. Pour the beef stock and red wine vinegar.
3. Allow stewing for 20 minutes till the stock and vinegar evaporate. Add thyme and green beans and cook for another 5 minutes. Use a slotted spoon to dish out the mixture and set aside.
4. Take a large saucepan and fill two-third of it with water. Cover the pan and heat till the water begins to boil. Add the cauliflower florets to boiling water. Simmer for about 7 minutes until it tenders.
5. Discard the cooking water carefully.
6. Add butter, pepper, and salt to the saucepan containing drained cauliflower.
7. Mash the tendered cauliflower by stick blender. Add egg yolks to the mashed cauliflower and mix well.
8. Preheat the oven to 350°F. Grease the baking dish with butter and transfer the minced beef mixture to it.

9. Top it with cauliflower mash. Garnish with oregano and paprika. Bake in preheated oven for half an hour or until the top starts to brown. Serve immediately or refrigerate for up to 7 days.

Nutrition:

36g Fat 18g Protein 4g Net Carbs 420 Calories

Pan Fried Spinach Stuffed Chicken

Preparation Time: 10 minutes

Cooking Time: 20 minutes

Serving: 2

Ingredients:

- 1 tbsp. mozzarella cheese (grated)

- 2 tbsp. cream cheese

- 1 chicken breast (boneless)

- 1 tbsp. onion (chopped)

- Oil as needed

- 1 tbsp. butter

- 1/2 cup spinach (chopped)

- Salt to taste

- Pepper to taste

Directions:

1. Place a pan over medium-high heat and add butter. Add onions and spinach, allow to cook for two minutes or until cooked thoroughly. Add in the cream cheese to the pan, mix well to combine. Allow simmering for two minutes.

2. Lay the chicken flat on your cutting board. Use a sharp knife to deep cut a pocket through chicken breast. Flavor both sides of chicken with salt and pepper. Spoon the shredded cheese and spinach mixture into the pocket.

3. Fold and seal the chicken breast with toothpicks. Place a skillet over medium-high heat and add olive oil. Cover the pan with a lid and cook the chicken for 8 minutes or until golden. Cut through the middle and serve hot.

Nutrition:

15g Fat 27g Protein 255Calories

Keto Chicken Tenders

Preparation Time: 10 minutes

Cooking Time: 30 minutes

Serving: 6

Ingredients:

- 1 egg
- 1 lb. chicken breast tenders
- 1 tbsp. heavy whipping cream
- 6 oz. buffalo sauce
- 1 cup almond flour
- Salt to taste
- Pepper to taste

Directions:

1. Preheat the oven to 350°F. Marinate the chicken tenders with salt and pepper. Crack the egg into a small bowl and beat it with heavy cream. Mix the almond flour with salt and pepper in a zip-top bag or mixing bowl.

2. Dip the marinated tender in the egg and then in the almond flour. Repeat the process with all tenders. You can also coat the tenders by shaking them in a Ziploc bag filled with almond flour. Ensure the tenders are well coated with almond flour.

3. Use the fork to place tenders on a baking sheet greased with oil. Place the sheet in the oven and allow to bake for 30 minutes or until the crust browns. Remove from the oven and allow to cool. Add buffalo sauce and tenders in a Tupperware container and shake gently for proper coating. Transfer to the serving plate and enjoy the delicious chicken tenders.

Nutrition:

14.7g Fat 29.3g Protein 285 Calories

Low-Carb Salmon Tray Bake

Preparation Time: 5 minutes

Cooking Time: 15 minutes Serving: 2

Ingredients:

- 2 medium salmon fillets
- 1 bunch broccolini
- 1 tbsp. extra virgin olive oil
- 2 tsp. whole-grain mustard
- 4 tbsp. Paleo mayonnaise
- 2 tsp. Dijon mustard
- Salt, to taste
- Black pepper, to taste
- Lemon wedges, to serve

Directions:

1. Preheat the oven to 200°C. Lay the broccolini on a cutting board and trim off the inedible parts – place in a baking tray and drizzle with olive oil. Pat the salmon fillets, and sprinkle the top with Dijon and whole-grain mustard.

2. Lay the salmon and lemon wedges with broccolini in the tray – season with salt and pepper. Bake for about 10 minutes until salmon is evenly-cooked, and broccolini turns tender-crisp. Serve instantly with mayonnaise or store in the refrigerator for one day.

Nutrition:

42.5g Fat 34.3g Protein 552 Calories

Zesty Low-Carb Chicken Tacos

Preparation Time: 15 minutes

Cooking Time: 35 minutes

Serving: 4

Ingredients:

Tortillas

- 3/4 cup egg whites
- 1/3 cup water
- 1/3 cup water
- 1/4 cup coconut flour

- 1/4 cup almond flour
- 2 tbsp. avocado oil
- 1/2 tsp. salt

Filling

- 1 lime
- 2 cups lettuce

- 1 avocado
- 1 lb. chicken breast

Directions:

1. Preheat the oven to 400°F and line a baking dish with parchment paper. Place the chicken on a baking dish and bake for 30 minutes or until fork-tender. Add water, coconut flour, egg whites, almond flour, salt and oil in a mixing bowl. Whisk together to combine.

2. Leave the batter to rest for 10 minutes till all the ingredients absorb well. Place a skillet over medium-high heat and grease with avocado oil. Take 1/4 cup of batter and add to the skillet. Spread the mixture with a wooden spoon.

3. Cook each side for about 4 minutes, flipping the sides occasionally. Remove from the heat once cooked thoroughly. Prepare all four tortillas by the same process. Place each tortilla on a separate parchment sheet and allow cooling. Slice the lettuce, avocado, and lime. Add the lettuce and avocado to the chicken and season with lime. Stuff the tortillas with chicken and lettuce filling.

Nutrition:

22g Fat 30g Protein 348 Calories

Keto Chicken Doner Kebabs

Preparation Time: 20 minutes

Cooking Time: 50 minutes

Serving: 4

Ingredients:

- 4 low carb tortillas
- 1-pound chicken thighs
- 1 tsp. paprika powder
- 1 tsp. cumin powder
- 1 tsp. ground coriander
- 1 tbsp. olive oil
- 1 tbsp. lemon juice
- 2 garlic cloves (minced)
- 2 tbsp. hot sauce
- 4 shreds of cheddar cheese
- 4 tbsp. keto garlic sauce
- 1 cup shredded lettuce
- 2 serves keto Lebanese salad (tabbouleh)
- 1/2 tsp. ground pepper
- 1/2 tsp. onion powder
- 1 tsp. salt

Directions:

1. Take a large bowl and add chicken, lemon juice, garlic, oil, and all the spices. Marinate the chicken by keeping it in the fridge for 3 hours. Refrigerate overnight for better results. Preheat the oven to 390°F.

2. Brush the metal skewers with oil and assemble the marinated chicken on them. Place the prepared skewers on the grill rack lined with foil. Make sure the chicken is not touching the bottom. Flip the skewers periodically and bake for an hour or 50 minutes. Make sure the meat is cooked through.

3. Put the chicken aside and prepare kebabs. Take a tortilla wrap and fill it with tabbouleh, cheddar cheese, garlic sauce, and lettuce. Fill all four wraps equally with the same ingredients. Sliver the chicken and add to the wraps. Embellish with hot sauce and gently roll the wraps.

Nutrition:

38g Fat 33g Protein 538 Calories

Low-Carb Instant Pot Frittata

Preparation Time: 10 minutes

Cooking Time: 30 minutes Serving: 8

Ingredients:

Frittata

- 8 eggs
- 1/2 cup spinach (chopped)
- 1/4 cup red onion (chopped)
- 1/4 cup bell pepper (diced)
- 1/3 cup heavy whipping cream

- 1/2 cup cheddar cheese (shredded)
- Pinch of black pepper
- 1 tsp. chili powder
- 1 tsp. sea salt

Topping

- 1
- /4 cup red onion (chopped)
- 1 avocado
- 1 tomato (diced)

- 2 tbsp. spring onion (slivered)
- 1 pickled jalapeno pepper (crushed)
- 1/2 cup sour cream

Directions:

1. Take a large bowl and beat together the eggs and heavy cream. Add the black pepper, chili powder, salt, spinach, onion, bell pepper, and cheddar cheese. Give a good mix until all the ingredients blend.
2. Grease a 7-inch baking dish with olive oil and transfer the mixture into it.
3. Fill the bottom of the instant pot with 1 cup of water. Place a trivet over the pot to keep the baking dish above water. Secure the lid, and use the manual button to cook for 12 minutes on high pressure.
4. Leave for 15 minutes till the pressure releases naturally. Remove the lid, once the floating valve drops. Add in the chopped tomatoes, salt and red onion. Mix well. Top the frittata with avocado, sour cream, jalapenos, and spring onion. Slice and serve warm. Refrigerate the leftovers in an airtight container for up to 5 days.

Nutrition:

17.6g Fat 9.4g Protein 218 Calories

Balsamic Chicken Thighs

Preparation Time: 15 minutes

Cooking Time: 4 hours Servings: 8

Ingredients:

- 1 teaspoon garlic powder
- 1 teaspoon dried basil
- 1/2 teaspoon salt
- 1/2 teaspoon pepper
- 2 teaspoons dehydrated onion
- 4 garlic cloves minced
- 1 tablespoon extra-virgin olive oil
- 1/2 cup balsamic vinegar divided
- 8 chicken thighs boneless, skinless
- sprinkle of fresh chopped parsley

Directions:

1. Combine the first five dry spices in a small bowl and spread over chicken on both sides. Set aside.
2. Pour olive oil and garlic on the bottom of the slow-cooker. Pour in 1/4 cup balsamic vinegar. Place chicken on top.
3. Sprinkle remaining balsamic vinegar over the chicken. Cover and cook on high for 3 hours if you have a fairly new slow cooker. If you have an older slow cooker you may need to cook another hour. Sprinkle with fresh parsley on top to serve.

Nutrition:

285 calories 20g fat 2g fiber 18g protein

Chicken Marsala

Preparation Time: 15 minutes

Cooking Time: 5 hours and 20 minutes

Servings: 6

Ingredients:

- Cooking spray
- 1 1/2 lb. boneless skinless chicken breasts
- kosher salt
- Freshly ground black pepper
- 8 oz. Mushrooms, sliced
- 3 cloves garlic, minced
- 1 c. marsala wine (you can sub with low-sodium chicken broth in a pinch)
- 1/2 c. water
- 1/4 c. almond flour
- 2 tbsp. heavy cream, optional (to make the sauce creamier)
- 2 tbsp. chopped parsley
- Lemon wedges, for serving

Directions:

1. Spray inside of slow-cooker with cooking spray. Season chicken all over with salt and pepper and add to slow-cooker. Top with mushrooms and garlic then pour Marsala wine on top.
2. Cover and cook on low for 4 to 5 hours, until chicken is cooked through.
3. Remove cooked chicken breasts from slow-cooker. In a small bowl, whisk together water and almond flour and whisk into the sauce. Whisk in heavy cream, if using, then return chicken to slow-cooker. Cover and cook on high until the sauce have thickened, about 20 minutes more. Garnish with parsley and serve with lemon wedges.

Nutrition:

312 calories 5g fat 3g fiber 33 protein

Chicken Fajitas

Preparation Time: 10 minutes

Cooking Time: 3 hours

Servings: 6

Ingredients:

- 4 boneless, skinless chicken breasts
- 3 bell peppers, thinly sliced
- 1 onion, thinly sliced
- 1/2 (7-oz.) can diced tomatoes
- 2 tsp. cumin
- 1/2 tsp. red pepper flakes
- Kosher salt
- Freshly ground black pepper

Directions:

1. Place chicken, bell peppers, and onions in slow-cooker then pour over diced tomatoes. Season with cumin, red pepper flakes, salt, and pepper. Cook on low for 3 hours, or until chicken is cooked through.
2. Remove chicken from slow-cooker and slice into strips.
3. Serve fajitas in tortillas with desired toppings.

Nutrition:

354 calories

13g fat

2.3g fiber

41.2g protein

Spring Beef Bourguignon

Preparation Time: 10 minutes

Cooking Time: 6 hours Servings: 6

Ingredients:

- 4 lb. beef chuck roast, cut into chunks
- 3 tbsp. extra-virgin olive oil
- 1 c. red wine
- 1/2 c. beef broth
- 2 c. sliced baby bell mushrooms
- 2 large carrots, sliced into rounds
- 1 large onion, diced
- 2 cloves garlic, chopped
- 3 sprigs fresh thyme
- 3 sprigs fresh rosemary
- 1 tsp. salt - ½ tsp. pepper
- 1 bunch asparagus, trimmed and quartered
- Chopped fresh parsley, for serving

Directions:

1. Heat a large skillet over medium-high heat. While it heats, toss beef with oil. Sear beef in batches, 3 minutes per side. Between each batch, deglaze pan with some red wine, scraping up any bits with a wooden spoon.

2. Pour mixture into slow-cooker along with seared beef as it's done. To slow-cooker, add beef broth, mushrooms, carrots, onion, garlic, thyme, rosemary, salt, pepper and remaining red wine.

3. Cook on high 6 hours, until beef is tender. Thirty minutes before serving, remove herbs and add asparagus; cook until just tender. Garnish with parsley and serve.

Nutrition:

613 calories 39g fat 49g protein

Mexican Shredded Beef

Preparation Time: 10 minutes

Cooking Time: 9 hours

Servings: 10

Ingredients:

- 3 pounds beef chuck roast
- 1 onion, diced
- 4 garlic cloves, minced
- 2 tablespoons tomato paste
- Juice of one lime (1-2 tablespoons)
- 1 Tablespoon chili powder
- 1 teaspoon cumin
- 1 teaspoon paprika
- 1 teaspoon dried oregano
- 1 teaspoon kosher salt, plus more to taste
- 1/4 teaspoon red chili flakes

Directions:

1. Mix together the chili powder, cumin, paprika, salt, oregano and red chili flakes, set aside. Add the chopped onion and garlic to the slow cooker with the tomato paste, lime juice, and just 1-2 teaspoons of the spice mixture. Stir everything together until fully mixed.

2. Sprinkle the rest of the spices all over the chuck roast, patting to help it stick to the meat.

3. Place the meat on top of the onion mixture and set cook on low for 7-8 hours. Total cooking time will vary for different roasts.

4. After meat has cooked, use two forks to shred the meat, removing any large pieces of fat or gristle as you find them. (If the meat is still too tough to shred, it needs to be cooked a little longer. Cook for an additional 30-60 minutes and check it again.) Stir to mix well with the sauce. Cover and continue to cook on low for another 30-60 minutes.

5. Before serving stir well again to mix the meat with the sauce. Taste meat and season with more salt to taste.

Nutrition:

416 calories 27g fat 28g protein

Pork Tenderloin

Preparation Time: 10 minutes

Cooking Time: 8 hours Servings: 6

Ingredients:

Shredded pork:

- 3 lbs. Pork Tenderloin
- Salt/Pepper
- Olive Oil

- 1 Cup Chicken or Vegetable Stock
- 1/2 teaspoon Ground Sage

For blackberry sauce:

- 10 ounces Fresh Blackberries
- 1/4 Cup Balsamic Vinegar

- 1/4 Cup Olive Oil
- Pinch Salt

Directions:

1. Salt and pepper pork tenderloin. Sear pork in large pan over high heat. Oil the bottom of a 6qt slow cooker.

2. Transfer pork tenderloin to slow cooker. Add stock and sage.

3. Cook on low for 8-9 hours. (I do not recommend cooking on high as it can cause the pork to dry out). Remove pork from slow cooker and shred. It should be falling apart. Pulse blackberries in blender. Push blackberry mixture through mesh strainer. Discard seeds.

4. In a 3.5qt pot, bring blackberry pulp, vinegar, olive oil and salt to a boil. Reduce heat and simmer 15-20 minutes while whisking occasionally. Vigorously whisk the last 2-3 minutes.

5. Once the sauce reaches a syrupy consistency, set aside to cool and thicken for 10 minutes before serving.

Nutrition:

188 calories 11g fat 30g protein

Creamy Lemon Chicken

Preparation Time: 10 minutes

Cooking Time: 5 hours

Servings: 6

Ingredients:

- 5 chicken breasts boneless and skinless
- 6 tablespoons unsalted butter divided
- 1/2 teaspoon kosher salt
- 1/4 teaspoon coarse ground black pepper
- 1 teaspoon Italian seasoning
- 2 lemons juiced and zested
- 2 garlic cloves minced
- 1 cup half and half
- 1 tablespoon heavy cream.
- 1 tablespoon chicken base optional

Directions:

1. In a large cast iron skillet add 1 tablespoon of butter to melt on medium high heat. Add the kosher salt, black pepper and Italian seasoning to the chicken and add it to the pan.
2. Cook on each side for 4-6 minutes. Add the chicken to your slow cooker. Cover with lemon juice, lemon zest, garlic and the rest of the butter in pieces
3. Cook on low for 4 hours or on high for 2 hours. In a large measuring cup add the half and half, heavy cream and chicken base and whisk well. Add the liquid, mix, and cook an additional hour on high.

Nutrition:

465 calories 21g fat 50g protein

Asian Porkchops

Preparation Time: 10 minutes

Cooking Time: 6 hours

Servings: 5

Ingredients:

- 4 thick-cut boneless pork chops
- 1 small onion, chopped
- ½ c. low-sodium soy sauce
- 2 tbsp. Splenda
- ¼ tsp. ginger

Directions:

1. Add pork chops and onions to the crock pot. In a small bowl, mix soy sauce, Splenda and ginger. Pour over pork chops in the crock pot. Cook on low for 6 hours or high for 3-4 hours.

2. May need to cook a little longer if your chops are frozen.

Nutrition:

306 calories 15g fat 24g protein

Sausage and Peppers

Preparation Time: 10 minutes

Cooking Time: 6 hours

Servings: 6

Ingredients:

- 5 to 6 medium cloves garlic finely chopped
- 2 large yellow onions halved and thinly sliced
- 4 green bell peppers halved from top to bottom, cleaned and thinly sliced
- 1 tablespoon kosher salt
- 1 teaspoon Italian Seasoning
- 1/4 teaspoon dried oregano
- 1/2 teaspoon crushed red pepper flakes
- 28 ounce can unsalted crushed tomatoes
- 1/4 cup cold water
- 1 bay leaf
- 1 3/4 to 2 pounds uncooked Italian Sausage Links Mild or Spicy
- chopped Italian parsley for serving optional

Directions:

1. Finely chop garlic. Remove the chopped garlic and onion to the slow cooker Slice bell peppers in half from top to bottom. Remove the ribs and any seeds. Add the sliced bell peppers to the slow cooker along with the salt, Italian Seasoning, dried oregano, crushed red pepper flakes, 1/4 cup cold water and 1 can have crushed tomatoes. Toss until well coated and liquid is evenly distributed.
2. Remove about half of the peppers and onion mixture to a bowl. Bury the uncooked sausages in the middle and return the peppers and onions back to the slow cooker to cover the sausage. Add the bay leaf. Cover, set to low and cook for 6 hours.
3. The onions and peppers will give off a lot of water as they cook which will make the sauce liquid and spoon-able so don't stress that there isn't enough liquid. Top with some chopped parsley, serve hot and enjoy!

Nutrition:

381 calories 23g fat 33g protein

Low-Carb Beef Short Ribs

Preparation Time: 15 minutes

Cooking Time: 4 hours

Servings: 12

Ingredients:

- 4 lbs. boneless or bone in, beef short ribs cut crosswise into 2-inch pieces
- salt
- pepper
- 2 tbsp. olive oil
- 1 cup beef broth
- 1 cup onion chopped
- 3 cloves garlic minced
- 2 tbsp. Worcestershire sauce homemade
- 2 tbsp. tomato paste
- 1 cup red wine

Directions:

1. Heat the oil in a large skillet over medium high heat. Season one side of your short ribs generously with salt and pepper.

2. Place half of the ribs, seasoned side down onto the hot skillet and brown. Season the top of the ribs in the skillet with salt and pepper. Flip once the bottom is browned. Remove and set aside while browning the rest of the meat.

3. Add beef broth to slow cooker and place short ribs into. To the same skillet add your remaining ingredients and bring to a boil. Cook for 5 minutes or until onion is tender. Pour this over the ribs in the slow-cooker. Cover and cook on high 4-6 hours or low 8-10 hours.

Nutrition:

604 calories 34g fat 5g carbs 65g protein

SEAFOOD RECIPES

Entertaining Salmon

Preparation Time: 20 minutes

Cooking Time: 16 minutes

Servings: 4

Ingredients:

For Salmon:

- 4 (6-oz.) skinless salmon fillets
- 2 tbsp. fresh lemon juice
- 2 tbsp. olive oil, divided
- 1 tbsp. unsalted butter

For Filling:

- 4 oz. cream cheese, softened
- ¼ C. Parmesan cheese, grated finely
- 4 oz. frozen spinach thawed and squeezed
- 2 tsp. garlic, minced

Directions:

1. Season each salmon fillet then, drizzle with lemon juice and 1 tbsp. of oil. Arrange the salmon fillets onto a smooth surface.

2. With a sharp knife, cut a pocket into each salmon fillet about ¾ of the way through.

3. For filling: in a bowl, add the cream cheese, Parmesan cheese, spinach, garlic, salt and black pepper and mix well.

4. Place about 1-2 tbsp. of spinach mixture into each salmon pocket and spread evenly.

5. In a skillet, heat the remaining oil and butter over medium-high heat and cook the salmon fillets for about 6-8 minutes per side.

6. Remove the salmon fillets from heat and transfer onto the serving plates. Serve.

Nutrition:

438 Calories 2.4g Carbohydrates 38.1g Protein

Flavors Infused Salmon

Preparation Time: 15 minutes

Cooking Time: 15 minutes Servings: 2

Ingredients:

- 2 (6-oz.) salmon fillets
- 2 streaky bacon slices
- 4 tbsp. pesto

Directions:

1. Preheat the oven to 3500 F. Line a medium baking sheet with parchment paper. Wrap each salmon fillet with 1 bacon slice and then, secure with a wooden skewer.

2. Place 2 tbsp. of pesto in the center of each salmon fillet. Arrange the salmon fillets onto prepared baking sheet. Bake for about 15 minutes.

3. Remove the salmon fillets from oven and serve hot.

Nutrition:

517 Calories 2.4g Carbohydrates 46.7g Protein:

Tuna Fish Salad

Preparation Time: 5 minutes

Cooking Time: 10 minutes Servings: 1

Ingredient:

- 10 kalamata olives, pitted
- 1 small zucchini sliced lengthwise
- ½ diced avocado
- 2 cups of mixed greens
- 1 large diced tomato
- 1 sliced green onion
- 1 can chunk light tuna in water
- ¼ cup fresh parsley, chopped
- ½ cup fresh mint, chopped
- 1 tbsp. extra virgin olive oil
- 1 tbsp. balsamic vinegar
- ¼ tsp. fine sea salt
- ¾ tsp. black pepper, cracked

Directions:

1. Grill the zucchini slices on each side for a few minutes or as desired. Once cooked, cut it into bite-size pieces. Grab a large bowl and just put all the ingredients together in the container, mixing them together.

2. Serve while still fresh. This salad would taste best if eaten immediately so try not to have any leftovers.

Nutrition:

563 calories 30.9g total fat 37.5g carbohydrates

Mozzarella Tuna Melt

Preparation Time: 10 minutes

Cooking Time: 10 minutes Serving: 2

Ingredients

- 1 tablespoon olive oil
- 1/2 cup diced yellow onion
- 8 ounces canned tuna
- 1/4 cup mayonnaise
- 2 large eggs
- 2 ounces shredded mozzarella cheese
- 1 green onion

Directions

1. Warm-up oil in a skillet over medium heat. Cook onion for 5 minutes.
2. Strain the tuna then flake it into the skillet and stir in remaining ingredients.
3. Season well and cook for 2 minutes or until the cheese melts. Top with sliced green onion to serve.

Nutrition:

110 calories 10g fat 26g protein

Crabmeat Egg Scramble with White Sauce

Preparation Time: 10 minutes

Cooking Time: 15 minutes

Serving: 2

Ingredients

- 1 tbsp. olive oil
- 4 eggs
- 4 oz. crabmeat

Sauce:

- ¾ cup crème fraiche
- ½ cup chives, chopped
- ½ tsp. garlic powder

Directions

1. Scourge eggs with a fork in a bowl, and season with salt and black pepper.
2. Set a sauté pan over medium heat and warm olive oil. Add in the eggs and scramble them.
3. Stir in crabmeat and cook until cooked thoroughly. In a mixing dish, combine crème fraiche and garlic powder. Season with salt and sprinkle with chives. Serve the eggs with the white sauce.

Nutrition:

105 calories 9g fat 31g protein

Tuna Pickle Boats

Preparation Time: 40 minutes

Cooking Time: 0 minute

Serving: 4

Ingredients

- 1 (5-oz) can tuna, drained
- 2 large dill pickles
- ¼ tsp. lemon juice
- 2 tsp. mayonnaise
- ¼ tbsp. onion flakes
- 1 tsp. dill. chopped

Directions

1. Cut the pickles in half lengthwise. Spoon out the seeds to create boats; set aside.
2. Combine the mayonnaise, tuna, onion flakes, and lemon juice in a bowl. Fill each boat with tuna mixture. Sprinkle with dill and place in the fridge for 30 minutes before serving.

Nutrition:

311 calories 12g fat 4g protein

Salmon Salad with Lettuce & Avocado

Preparation Time: 5 minutes

Cooking Time: 0 minute

Serving: 3

Ingredients

- 2 slices smoked salmon
- 1 tsp. onion flakes
- 3 tbsp. mayonnaise
- 1 cup romaine lettuce
- 1 tbsp. lime juice
- 1 tbsp. extra virgin olive oil
- ½ avocado, sliced

Directions

1. Combine the salmon, mayonnaise, lime juice, olive oil, and salt in a small bowl; mix to combine well.
2. In a salad platter, arrange the shredded lettuce and onion flakes. Spread the salmon mixture over; top with avocado slices and serve.

Nutrition:

112 calories 6g fat 28g protein

Mackerel Lettuce Cups

Preparation Time: 10 minutes

Cooking Time: 20 minutes

Serving: 4

Ingredients

- 2 mackerel fillets
- 1 tbsp. olive oil
- 2 eggs
- 1 ½ cups water
- 1 tomato, seeded
- 2 tbsp. mayonnaise
- ½ head green lettuce

Directions

1. Preheat a grill pan over medium heat. Dash mackerel fillets with olive oil, and sprinkle with salt and black pepper. Add the fish to the preheated grill pan and cook on both sides for 6-8 minutes.

2. Bring the eggs to boil in salted water in a pot over medium heat for 10 minutes. Then, run the eggs in cold water, peel, and chop into small pieces. Transfer to a salad bowl.

3. Remove the mackerel fillets to the salad bowl. Include the tomatoes and mayonnaise; mix evenly with a spoon.

4. Layer two lettuce leaves each as cups and fill with two tablespoons of egg salad each.

Nutrition:

107 calories 14g fat 27g protein

Watercress & Shrimp Salad with Lemon Dressing

Preparation Time: 10 minutes

Cooking Time: 1 hour 10 minutes Serving: 2

Ingredients

- 1 cup watercress leaves
- 2 tbsp. capers
- ½ pound shrimp
- 1 tbsp. dill

Dressing:

- ¼ cup mayonnaise
- ½ tsp. apple cider vinegar
- ¼ tsp. sesame seeds
- 1 tbsp. lemon juice
- 2 tsp. stevia

Directions

1. Combine the watercress leaves, shrimp, and dill in a large bowl. Whisk together the mayonnaise, vinegar, sesame seeds, black pepper, stevia, and lemon juice in another bowl. Season with salt.
2. Drizzle dressing over and gently toss to combine; refrigerate for 1 hour. Top with capers to serve.

Nutrition: 101 calories 8g fat 21g protein

Salad of Prawns and Mixed Lettuce Greens

Preparation Time: 10 minutes

Cooking Time: 15 minutes

Serving: 3

Ingredients

- 2 cups mixed lettuce greens
- ¼ cup aioli
- 1 tbsp. olive oil
- ½ pound tiger prawns
- ½ tsp. Dijon mustard
- 1 tbsp. lemon juice

Directions

1. Season the prawns with salt and chili pepper. Fry in warm olive oil over medium heat for 3 minutes on each side until prawns are pink. Set aside. Add the aioli, lemon juice and mustard in a small bowl. Mix until smooth and creamy.

2. Place the mixed lettuce greens in a bowl and pour half of the dressing on the salad. Toss with 2 spoons until mixed, and add the remaining dressing. Divide salad among plates and serve with prawns.

Nutrition:

107 calories 4g fat 26g protein

VEGAN RECIPES

Italian Stuffed Mushrooms

Preparation Time: 10 minutes

Cooking Time: 35 minutes Servings: 4

Ingredients:

- 1-pound button mushrooms, stems removed
- 2 tablespoons coconut oil, melted
- 1-pound broccoli florets
- 1 Italian pepper, chopped
- 1 teaspoon Italian herb mix
- Salt and pepper, to taste
- 1 shallot, finely chopped
- 2 garlic cloves, minced
- 1 cup vegan parmesan

Directions:

1. Parboil the broccoli in a large pot of salted water until crisp-tender, about 6 minutes. Mash the broccoli florets with a potato masher. In a saucepan, melt the coconut oil over a moderately-high heat. Once hot, cook the shallot, garlic, and pepper until tender and fragrant. Season with the spices and add in the broccoli.

2. Fill the mushroom cups with the broccoli mixture and bake in the preheated oven at 365 degrees F for about 10 minutes. Top with the vegan parmesan and bake for 10 minutes more or until it melts.

Nutrition:

206 Calories 13.4g Fat 12.7g Protein 4g Fiber

One-Pot Mushroom Stroganoff

Preparation Time: 10 minutes

Cooking Time: 25 minutes

Serving: 4

Ingredients:

- 2 tablespoons canola oil
- 1 parsnip, chopped
- 1 cup fresh brown mushrooms, sliced
- 1 cup onions, chopped
- 2 garlic cloves, pressed
- 1/2 cup celery rib, chopped
- 1 teaspoon Hungarian paprika
- 3 ½ cups roasted vegetable broth
- 1 cup tomato puree
- 1 tablespoon flaxseed meal
- 2 tablespoons sherry wine
- 1 rosemary sprig, chopped
- 1/2 teaspoon dried basil
- 1/2 teaspoon dried oregano

Directions:

1. In a heavy-bottomed pot, heat the oil over a moderately-high flame. Cook the onion and garlic for 2 minutes or until tender and aromatic.

2. Add in the celery, parsnip, and mushrooms, and continue to cook until they've softened; reserve.

3. Add in the sherry wine to deglaze the bottom of your pot. Add in the seasonings, vegetable broth, and tomato puree.

4. Continue to simmer, partially covered, for 15 to 18 minutes. Add in the flaxseed meal and stir until the sauce has thickened.

Nutrition:

114 Calories 7.3g Fat

2.1g Protein 3.1g Fiber

Avocado with Pine Nuts

Preparation Time: 5 minutes

Cooking Time: 10 minutes Serving: 4

Ingredients:

- 2 avocados, pitted and halved
- 1 tablespoon coconut aminos
- 1/2 teaspoon garlic, minced
- 1 teaspoon fresh lime juice
- Salt and pepper, to taste
- 5 ounces pine nuts, ground
- 1 celery stalk, chopped

Directions:

1. Thoroughly combine the avocado pulp with the pine nuts, celery, garlic, fresh lime juice, and coconut aminos. Season with salt and pepper to taste.

2. Spoon the filling into the avocado halves.

Nutrition:

263 Calories 24.8g Fat 3.5g Protein 6.1g Fiber

Zucchini Noodles with Famous Cashew Parmesan

Preparation Time: 5 minutes

Cooking Time: 15 minutes

Serving: 4

Ingredients:

For Zoodles:

- 2 tablespoons canola oil

- 4 zucchinis, peeled and sliced into noodle-shape strands

- Salt and pepper, to taste

For Cashew Parmesan:

- 1/2 cup raw cashews

- 1/4 teaspoon onion powder

- 1 garlic clove, minced

- 2 tablespoons nutritional yeast

- Sea salt and pepper, to taste

Directions:

1. In a saucepan, heat the canola oil over medium heat; once hot, cook your zoodles for 1 minute or so, stirring frequently to ensure even cooking.

2. Season with salt and pepper to taste.

3. In your food processor, process all ingredients for the cashew parmesan. Toss the cashew parmesan with the zoodles and enjoy!

Nutrition:

145 Calories 10.6g Fat 5.5g Protein 1.6g Fiber

Cream of Broccoli Soup

Preparation Time: 5 minutes

Cooking Time: 15 minutes

Serving: 4

Ingredients:

- 1-pound broccoli, cut into small florets
- 8 ounces baby spinach
- 4 cups roasted vegetable broth
- 2 tablespoons olive oil
- 1 yellow onion, chopped
- 2 garlic cloves, minced
- 1/2 cup coconut milk
- Salt and pepper, to taste
- 2 tablespoons parsley, chopped

Directions:

1. Heat the oil in a soup pot over a moderately-high flame. Then, sauté the onion and garlic until they're tender and fragrant.

2. Add in the broccoli, spinach, and broth; bring to a rolling boil. Immediately turn the heat to a simmer.

3. Pour in the coconut milk, salt, pepper, and parsley; continue to simmer, partially covered, until cooked through.

4. Puree your soup with an immersion blender.

Nutrition:

252 Calories 20.3g Fat 8.1g Protein 4.5g Fiber

Swiss Chard Chips with Avocado Dip

Preparation Time: 10 minutes

Cooking Time: 20 minutes Serving: 6

Ingredients:

- 1 tablespoon coconut oil
- Sea salt and pepper, to taste
- 2 cups Swiss chard, cleaned

Avocado Dip:

- 3 ripe avocados, pitted and mashed
- 2 garlic cloves, finely minced
- 2 tablespoons extra-virgin olive oil
- 2 teaspoons lemon juice
- Salt and pepper, to taste

Directions:

1. Toss the Swiss chard with the coconut oil, salt, and pepper. Bake the Swiss chard leaves in the preheated oven at 310 degrees F for about 10 minutes until the edges brown but are not burnt.
2. Thoroughly combine the ingredients for the avocado dip.

Nutrition:

269 Calories

26.7g Fat

2.3g Protein

4.1g Fiber

Banana Blueberry Smoothie

Preparation Time: 5 minutes

Cooking Time: 0 minutes

Serving: 4

Ingredients:

- 1/2 cup fresh blueberries

- 1/2 banana, peeled and sliced

- 1/2 cup water

- 1 ½ cups coconut milk

- 1 tablespoon vegan protein powder, zero carbs

Directions:

1. Blend all ingredients until creamy and uniform.

Nutrition:

247 Calories 21.7g Fat 2.6g Protein 3g Fiber

Cajun Artichoke with Tofu

Preparation Time: 15 minutes

Cooking Time: 30 minutes

Serving: 4

Ingredients:

- 1-pound artichokes, trimmed and cut into pieces
- 2 tablespoons coconut oil, room temperature
- 1 block tofu, pressed and cubed
- 1 teaspoon fresh garlic, minced
- 1 teaspoon Cajun spice mix
- 1 Spanish pepper, chopped
- 1/4 cup vegetable broth
- Salt and pepper, to taste

Directions:

1. Parboil your artichokes in a pot of lightly salted water for 13 to 15 minutes or until they're crisp-tender; drain.
2. In a large saucepan, melt the coconut oil over medium-high heat; fry the tofu cubes for 5 to 6 minutes or until golden-brown.
3. Add in the garlic, Cajun spice mix, Spanish pepper, broth, salt, and pepper. Add in the reserved artichokes and continue to cook until for 5 minutes more.

Nutrition:

138 Calories 8.9g Fat 6.4g Protein 5g Fiber

Mushroom and Cauliflower Medley

Preparation Time: 15 minutes

Cooking Time: 30 minutes Serving: 4

Ingredients:

- 8 ounces brown mushrooms, halved
- 1 head cauliflower, cut into florets
- 1/4 cup olive oil
- 1/2 teaspoon turmeric powder
- 1 teaspoon garlic, smashed
- 1 cup tomato, pureed
- Salt and pepper, to taste

Directions:

1. Toss all ingredients in a lightly oiled baking pan.
2. Roast the vegetable in the preheated oven at 380 degrees F for 25 to 30 minutes.

Nutrition:

113 Calories 6.7g Fat 5g Protein 2.7g Fiber

Spicy and Peppery Fried Tofu

Preparation Time: 10 minutes

Cooking Time: 20 minutes

Serving: 2

Ingredients:

- 2 bell peppers, deveined and sliced
- 1 chili pepper, deveined and sliced
- 1 ½ tablespoons almond meal
- Salt and pepper, to taste
- 1 teaspoon ginger-garlic paste
- 1 teaspoon onion powder
- 6 ounces extra-firm tofu, pressed and cubed
- 1/2 teaspoon ground bay leaf
- 1 tablespoon sesame oil

Directions:

1. Toss your tofu, with almond meal, salt, pepper, ginger-garlic paste, onion powder, ground bay leaf.
2. In a sauté pan, heat the sesame oil over medium-high heat.
3. Fry the tofu cubes along with the peppers for about 6 minutes.

Nutrition:

223 Calories 15.9g Fat 15.6g Protein 3.3g Fiber

Colorful Creamy Soup

Preparation Time: 10 minutes

Cooking Time: 25 minutes Serving: 6

Ingredients:

- 2 cups Swiss chard, torn into pieces
- Sea salt and pepper, to taste
- 2 thyme sprigs, chopped
- 2 teaspoons sesame oil
- 1 onion, chopped - 2 bay leaves
- 6 cups vegetable broth
- 1 cup grape tomatoes, chopped
- 1 cup almond milk, unflavored
- 1 teaspoon garlic, minced
- 2 celery stalks, chopped
- 1 zucchini, chopped
- 1/2 cup scallions, chopped

Directions:

1. In a heavy bottomed pot, heat the sesame oil in over a moderately-high heat. Sauté the onion, garlic, and celery, until they've softened. Add in the zucchini, Swiss chard, salt, pepper, thyme, bay leaves, broth, and tomatoes; bring to a rapid boil. Turn the heat to a simmer.

2. Leave the lid slightly ajar and continue to simmer for about 13 minutes. Add in the almond milk and scallions; continue to cook for 4 minutes more or until thoroughly warmed.

Nutrition:

142 Calories 11.4g Fat 2.9g Protein 1.3g Fiber

Tofu Stuffed Zucchini

Preparation Time: 20 minutes

Cooking Time: 50 minutes Serving: 4

Ingredients:

- 4 zucchinis, cut into halves lengthwise and scoop out the pulp
- 6 ounces firm tofu, drained and crumbled
- 2 garlic cloves, pressed
- 1/2 cup onions, chopped
- 1 tablespoon olive oil
- 1 cup tomato puree
- 1 tablespoon nutritional yeast
- 2 ounces pecans, chopped
- 1/4 teaspoon curry powder
- Sea salt and pepper, to taste

Directions:

1. In a saucepan, heat the olive oil over a moderately-high heat; cook the tofu, garlic, and onion for about 5 minutes.
2. Stir in the tomato puree and scooped zucchini pulp; add all seasonings and continue to cook for a further 5 to 6 minutes.
3. Spoon the filling into the zucchini "shells" and arrange them in a lightly greased baking dish.
4. Bake in the preheated oven at 365 degrees F for 25 to 30 minutes. Top with nutritional yeast and pecans nuts; bake for a further 5 minutes.

Nutrition:

208 Calories 14.4g Fat 6.5g Protein 4.3g Fiber

Broccoli Masala

Preparation Time: 5 minutes

Cooking Time: 15 minutes

Serving: 4

Ingredients:

- 1/4 cup sesame oil

- 1-pound broccoli florets

- 1/2 teaspoon Garam Masala

- 1 tablespoon Kasuri Methi (dried fenugreek leaves)

- 1 Badi Elaichi (black cardamom)

- 1 teaspoon garlic, pressed

- Salt and pepper, to taste

Directions:

1. Parboil the broccoli for 6 to 7 minutes until it is crisp-tender.

2. Heat the sesame oil in a wok or saucepan until sizzling. Once hot, cook your broccoli for 3 to 4 minutes. Add in the other ingredients and give it a quick stir.

3. Adjust the spices to suit your taste.

Nutrition:

100 Calories 8.2g Fat 3.7g Protein 4g Fiber

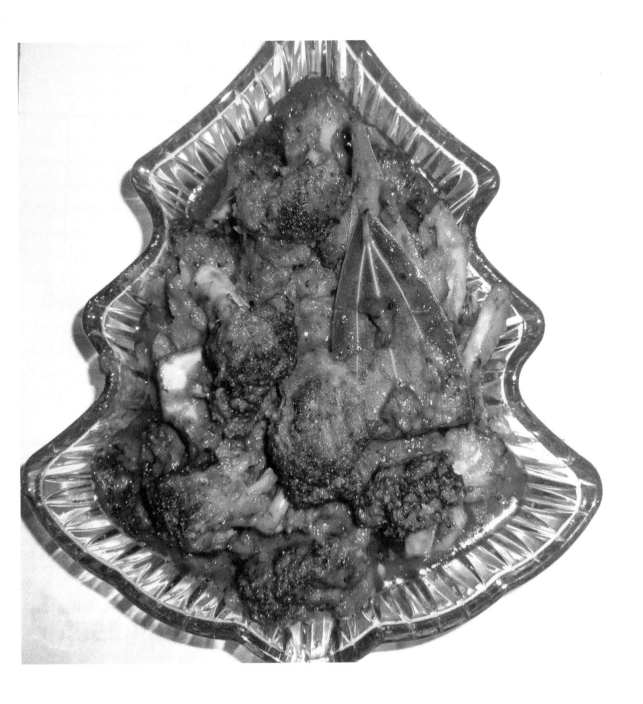

Italian-Style Tomato Crisps

Preparation Time: 10 minutes

Cooking Time: 5 hours

Serving: 6

Ingredients:

- 1 tablespoon Italian spice mix
- 1 ½ pounds Romano tomatoes, sliced
- 1/4 cup extra-virgin olive oil
- For Vegan Parmesan:
- 1/4 cup sunflower seeds
- Salt and pepper, to taste
- 1/4 teaspoon dried dill weed
- 1 teaspoon garlic powder
- 1/4 cup sesame seeds
- 1 tablespoon nutritional yeast

Directions:

1. Process all ingredients for the vegan parmesan in your food processor.
2. Toss the sliced tomatoes with the extra-virgin olive oil, Italian spice mix, and vegan parmesan.
3. Arrange the tomato slices on a parchment-lined baking sheet in a single layer. Bake at 220 degrees F about 5 hours.

Nutrition:

161 Calories 14g Fat 4.6g Protein 2.6g Fiber

Lebanese Asparagus with Baba Ghanoush

Preparation Time: 15 minutes

Cooking Time: 45 minutes

Serving: 6

Ingredients:

- 1/4 cup sesame oil
- 1 ½ pounds asparagus spears, med
- 1/2 teaspoon red pepper flakes
- Salt and pepper, to taste
- For Baba Ghanoush:
- 2 tablespoons fresh lime juice
- 2 teaspoons olive oil
- 1/2 cup onion, chopped
- 3/4-pound eggplant
- 1 teaspoon garlic, minced
- 1 tablespoon sesame paste
- 1/2 teaspoon allspice
- 1/4 teaspoon ground nutmeg
- 1/4 cup fresh parsley leaves, chopped
- Salt and ground black pepper, to taste

Directions:

1. Toss the asparagus spears with sesame oil, salt, and pepper. Arrange the asparagus spears on a foil-lined baking pan.

2. Roast in the preheated oven at 380 degrees F for 8 to 10 minutes.

3. Meanwhile, make your Baba Ghanoush. Bake eggplants in the preheated oven at 420 degrees F for 25 to 30 minutes; discard the skin and stems. In a saucepan, heat 2 the olive oil over a moderately-high heat. Cook the onion and garlic until tender and fragrant; heat off.

4. Add the roasted eggplant, sautéed onion mixture, sesame paste, lime juice, and spices to your blender or food processor. Pulse until creamy and smooth.

Nutrition:

149 Calories 12.1g Fat 3.6g Protein 4.6g Fiber

Garlic Mozzarella Bread

Preparation Time: 20 minutes

Cooking Time: 65 minutes Serving: 8

Ingredients:

- 1 cup vegan mozzarella
- 1 cup almond flour
- ½ medium onion (diced)
- 4 tbsp. ground flaxseed
- 3 tbsp. olive oil
- ½ cup water
- 1 tbsp. Italian herbs
- ½ tsp. baking powder
- 2 garlic cloves (minced)
- Optional: ¼ cup black olives

Directions:

1. Preheat the oven to 350°F/175°C and line a large loaf pan with parchment paper. In a small bowl, combine the water with the ground flaxseed. Let the flaxseed soak for about 10 minutes.

2. Put the soaked seeds in a food processor with all the other ingredients, and pulse until they are combined into a smooth batter. Scrape the sides of the food processor if necessary. Transfer the batter onto the loaf pan and let the mixture sit for a few minutes.

3. Put the loaf pan in the oven and bake the bread for 50 minutes, until the bread is firm and browned on top. Take the loaf pan out of the oven and allow the bread to cool down completely.

4. Transfer the bread to a cutting board and slice it into 8 slices. Serve and enjoy!

5. Alternatively, store the bread in an airtight container in the fridge and consume within 4 days. Store for a maximum of 60 days in the freezer and thaw at room temperature before serving.

Nutrition:

256 Calories 23.5 g. Fat 6.6 g. Protein

Truffle Parmesan Bread

Preparation Time: 20 minutes

Cooking Time: 65 minutes

Serving: 8

Ingredients:

- 1 cup truffle parmesan cheese
- 1 cup almond flour
- ½ cup button mushrooms (diced)
- 2 tbsp. soy sauce
- ½ medium onion (finely chopped)
- ½ cup ground flaxseed
- 4 tbsp. olive oil
- ½ cup water
- 1 tsp. dried thyme
- 1 tsp. dried basil
- 1 tsp. black pepper
- ½ tsp. baking powder

Directions:

1. Preheat the oven to 350°F/175°C and line a large loaf pan with parchment paper. In a small bowl, combine the water with the ground flaxseed. Let the flaxseed soak for about 10 minutes.
2. Meanwhile, put a medium-sized frying pan over medium-high heat and add a tablespoon of olive oil. When the oil is warm, add the chopped onions, mushrooms, and soy sauce to the frying pan and stir-fry until the mushrooms and onion have softened.
3. Put the flaxseed, stir-fried ingredients, and all remaining ingredients in a food processor and pulse until all ingredients are combined into a smooth mixture. Scrape down the sides of the food processor if necessary.
4. Transfer the mixture into the loaf pan and let the mixture sit for a few minutes. Put the loaf pan in the oven and bake the bread for about 50 minutes, until the bread is firm and browned on top.
5. Take the loaf pan out of the oven and allow the bread to cool down completely. Transfer the bread to a cutting board and slice it into 8 slices. Serve warm or cold and enjoy!
6. Alternatively, store the bread in an airtight container in the fridge and consume within 4 days.
7. Store for a maximum of 60 days in the freezer and thaw at room temperature before serving.

Nutrition:

296 Calories 26.9 g. Fat 7.7 g. Protein

Truffle Parmesan Salad

Preparation Time: 10 minutes

Cooking Time: 15 minutes

Serving: 4

Ingredients:

- 4 cups kale (chopped)
- ½ cup truffle parmesan cheese
- 1 tsp. Dijon mustard
- 2 tbsp. olive oil
- 2 tbsp. lemon juice
- Salt and pepper to taste
- Optional: 2 tbsp. water

Directions:

1. Rinse the kale with cold water, then drain the kale and put it into a large bowl. In a medium-sized bowl, mix the remaining ingredients into a dressing. Pour the dressing over the kale and stir gently to cover the kale evenly.

2. Transfer the large bowl to the fridge and allow the salad to chill for up to one hour – doing so will guarantee a better flavor. Alternatively, the salad can be served right away. Enjoy!

3. Alternatively, store the salad in the fridge using an airtight container and consume within 2 days.

Nutrition:

199 Calories 16.6 g Fat 3.5 g. Protein 1.9 g. Fiber

Cashew Siam Salad

Preparation Time: 10 minutes

Cooking Time: 15 minutes

Serving: 4

Ingredients:

Salad:

- 4 cups baby spinach (rinsed, drained)
- ½ cup pickled red cabbage

Dressing:

- 1-inch piece ginger (finely chopped)
- 1 tsp. chili garlic paste
- 1 tbsp. soy sauce
- ½ tbsp. rice vinegar
- 1 tbsp. sesame oil
- 3 tbsp. avocado oil
- Toppings:
- ½ cup raw cashews (unsalted)
- Optional: ¼ cup fresh cilantro (chopped)

Directions:

1. Put the spinach and red cabbage in a large bowl. Toss to combine and set the salad aside. Toast the cashews in a frying pan over medium-high heat, stirring occasionally until the cashews are golden brown. This should take about 3 minutes. Turn off the heat and set the frying pan aside.

2. Mix all the dressing ingredients in medium-sized bowl and use a spoon to mix them into a smooth dressing. Pour the dressing over the spinach salad and top with the toasted cashews.

3. Toss the salad to combine all ingredients and transfer the large bowl to the fridge. Allow the salad to chill for up to one hour – doing so will guarantee a better flavor.

4. Alternatively, the salad can be served right away, topped with the optional cilantro. Enjoy!

5. Alternatively, store the salad in the fridge using an airtight container and consume within 2 days.

Nutrition:

236 Calories 21.6 g. Fat 4.2 g. Protein 1.3 g. Fiber

Avocado and Cauliflower Hummus

Preparation Time: 10 minutes

Cooking Time: 20 minutes

Serving: 2

Ingredients:

- 1 medium cauliflower (stem removed and chopped)
- 1 large Hass avocado (peeled, pitted, and chopped)
- ¼ cup extra virgin olive oil
- 2 garlic cloves
- ½ tbsp. lemon juice
- ½ tsp. onion powder
- Sea salt and ground black pepper to taste
- 2 large carrots (peeled and cut into fries, or use store-bought raw carrot fries)
- Optional: ¼ cup fresh cilantro (chopped)

Directions:

1. Preheat the oven to 450°F/220°C, and line a baking tray with aluminum foil. Put the chopped cauliflower on the baking tray and drizzle with 2 tablespoons of olive oil.

2. Roast the chopped cauliflower in the oven for 20-25 minutes, until lightly brown. Remove the tray from the oven and allow the cauliflower to cool down.

3. Add all the ingredients—except the carrots and optional fresh cilantro—to a food processor or blender, and blend the ingredients into a smooth hummus. Transfer the hummus to a medium-sized bowl, cover, and put it in the fridge for at least 30 minutes.

4. Take the hummus out of the fridge and, if desired, top it with the optional chopped cilantro and more salt and pepper to taste; serve with the carrot fries, and enjoy!

5. Alternatively, store it in the fridge in an airtight container, and consume within 2 days

Nutrition:

416 Calories 40.3g. Fat 3.3g. Protein 10.3g. Fiber

Conclusion

If you're eyeing for a diet that works and gives you the results you want, then it's time to take your health and performance to the next level. It is also one of the most effective ways to reduce appetite and feel full. It's also a natural heal for diabetes, epilepsy, and Alzheimer's disease.

This keto diet is a low-carbohydrate, high-fat diet that increases your body's ability to burn fat as fuel.

The ketogenic diet main purpose is to cause your body to make ketones, which are compounds produced by the liver used as an alternative fuel source for your body instead of glucose (sugar). These ketones then serve as a fuel source all over the body, especially for the brain.

In less than 5 years, the keto diet has gone from a notorious fad diet to a well-respected high-protein health and wellness regimen. An increasing amount of people are deciding on living without carbohydrates. They rely solely on fat-forming foods like meat, fish, eggs, cheese, butter, and coconut oil for their caloric intake. This trend has been gaining ground for more than 30 years with people following such diets as Atkins. The reason for this recent spike in popularity can be attributed partially to the 2014 documentary The Carbohydrate Addict, which focuses on Dr. Robert Atkins' theory that carbohydrates play a central role in heart disease.

Not long after its release, the ketogenic diet was used as the backbone of a new trend known as "ketogenic" or "low carb" diets. These low-carb diets claim that by restricting carbohydrates from your daily meal plan, your body will become efficient at burning fat as fuel instead of glucose. The purpose of following such a regimen is to create your own "ketogenic" state wherein your body will naturally become efficient at burning fat stored within your liver and muscles for energy instead of carbohydrates.

The first thing people should be prepared for is the signs of the body-switching over to ketosis. These include bad breath, weight loss, appetite decrease, and potential weakness in the beginning stages. It is normal to have these reactions while doing the keto diet. It can also be helpful to be familiar with the keto flu's signs and symptoms, which can affect people at varying severities. Finally, they should have an idea of how long they will need to stay on a diet to achieve their desired results. Some people choose to do standard keto until they reach their weight loss goals and then choose a less vigorous form of the diet to keep the pounds off.

For people who have stomach issues when starting the diet, switching to fats that are easier to digest can be a smart move for the beginning stages. Adding fiber to the diet can also help regulate the gut and ease those uncomfortable symptoms.

After making it through the keto flu, here are the benefits of the diet. Some people decide to stay on the meal plan long term. Although it is not recommended to do full keto for longer than a year, keeping some form of the diet long-term can help to ensure the goals met are not lost. To ensure that staying on a diet is simple and easy, people should focus on eating quality fats that smoothly help their brain and body function. If the body doesn't have to work hard to digest food, the person will usually have more energy and feel better overall.